KU-476-792

Peak District: **Pub** Walks

Text: *Dennis Kelsall*
Series editor: *Tony Bowerman*
Photographs: *Dennis and Jan Kelsall, James Grant Photography/www.jamesgphotography.co.uk, James Pictures/www.jamespictures.co.uk, Steven Wood, fwdmotion.co.uk, Shutterstock, Dreamstime*

Design: *Carl Rogers*

Northern Eye Books
ISBN 978-1-908632-09-8

A CIP catalogue record for this book is available from the British Library.

Printed in the UK by Charlesworth Press

Cover: *The Peacock, Bakewell (Walk 3)*

Important Advice: The routes described in this book are undertaken at the reader's own risk. Walkers should take into account their level of fitness, wear suitable footwear and clothing, and carry food and water. It is also advisable to take the relevant OS map with you in case you get lost and leave the area covered by our maps.

Whilst every care has been taken to ensure the accuracy of the route directions, the publishers cannot accept responsibility for errors or omissions, or for changes in the details given. Nor can the publisher and copyright owners accept responsibility for any consequences arising from the use of this book.

If you find any inaccuracies in either the text or maps, please write or email us at the address below. Thank you.

This edition published in 2016 by
Northern Eye Books Limited
Northern Eye Books, Tattenhall, Cheshire CH3 9PX
Email: tony@northerneyebooks.com
For sales enquiries, please call 01928 723 744

www.northerneyebooks.co.uk
www.top10walks.co.uk

 Twitter: @Northerneyeboo
@Top10walks

Contents

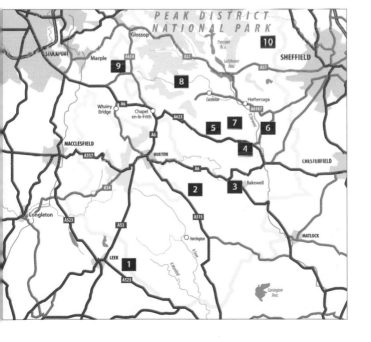

Britain's First National Park

CREATED IN 1951, THE PEAK DISTRICT NATIONAL PARK extends over six counties and is the second most visited of Britain's National Parks. Its highest point lies upon the seemingly remote Kinder plateau, where a mass trespass in 1932 marked the turning point in a long and sometimes bitter campaign that led to the creation of Britain's National Parks and the open access we enjoy today.

The high, peaty moorlands of the northern Dark Peak are founded on gritstone, their stark grandeur accentuated by impressive, weather-worn tors and edges. The moors extend out of the Pennines in two horns that enclose the limestone plateau of the White Peak, an upland pasture cleft by narrow gorges and dales. The transition between the two is abrupt and each has a distinctive character and beauty all its own: the wild openness of the north contrasting with the more intimate southern landscape, dotted with small villages and criss-crossed by old lanes.

The Old Nag's Head in Edale is the official start of the Pennine Way

Pubs in the Peak District

Ever since rambling became a recognised pastime, country pubs have been magnets for walkers. Whether a lunch time stop along the way or a final destination for the day, the promise of a thirst-quenching pint or a hearty meal are, for many, an integral part of the day. Many of Peakland's inns have their origins in serving the jaggers and stockmen who travelled the lonely upland routes. Today, they serve not only the locals but also the growing influx of recreational visitors. Long live the Peak District pub.

> "… not forgetting the ale, which everywhere exceeded, if possible, what was passed — as if the farther north, the better the liquor."

Daniel Defoe, 1722

TOP 10 **Walks:** The Best Pub Walks

THERE IS NO SHORTAGE OF EXCELLENT PUBS in the Peak District. In fact, pop into any and you'll rarely be disappointed. Likewise, there is no difficulty in devising pleasing circular walks, and this collection combines the best of both worlds in ten enjoyable rambles. Each short, circular walk explores a different aspect of the Peakland landscape and is crafted to create and then satisfy a healthy outdoor appetite. And, of course, a respectable thirst.

Ye Olde Royal Oak, Wetton — page 8

The Bull's Head, Monyash — page 1[?]

The Peacock, Bakewell — page 18

The Bridge Inn, Calver — page 2[?]

The vast, water-worn entrance to Thor's Cave

Ye Olde Royal Oak
Wetton

What to expect:
Tracks, field paths and some quiet lanes; steady climb back to the village

Distance/time: 6km/ 3¾ miles. Allow 2 hours

Start: Car park at south-western corner of Wetton village

Grid ref: SK 109 551

Ordnance Survey Map: Explorer OL24 Peak District: White Peak area: *Buxton, Bakewell, Matlock & Dove Dale*

The Pub: Ye Olde Royal Oak, Wetton, near Ashbourne, Staffordshire DE6 2AF | 01335 310287 | www.royaloakwetton.co.uk

Walk outline: The Manifold Valley and its many caves have attracted visitors since Victorian times, and remains popular with walkers and cyclists today. This ramble takes a roundabout route passing the spectacular outcrop of Beeston Tor, rearing above the valley. It later climbs through woodland to the impressive mouth of Thor's Cave before returning across the fields to the village and its pub.

Behind the church in the heart of Wetton, Ye Olde Royal Oak dates back to the 1760s and is a traditional and unpretentious village local where walkers, cyclists and campers are particularly welcome.

Ye Olde Royal Oak

▶ Ye Olde Royal Oak at a glance

Open: Wed-Sun (daily during school holidays), 12-2pm (2.30pm at weekends) and 7-11pm

Brewery/company: Free house

Real ales: Varying selection of guest real ales

Food: Meals served during opening hours until 8.30pm (8.45pm Fri, 9pm Sat). Specials board, children's, vegetarian and snack options

Accommodation: Campsite and two-bedroom self-catering barn

Outside: Forecourt tables

Children & dogs: Well-behaved children and dogs on leads

The Walk

1. Turn right out of the car park and follow **Carr Lane** past a junction. After 800 metres/½ mile, watch for a gated gap stile on the right and bear left downfield to a gate and stile in the bottom corner.

2. Emerging onto **Larkstone Lane**, cross a cattle-grid and immediately turn through a gate on the left. Descend by the left wall to a gate and carry on along an old track that winds to the foot of **Beeston Tor**.

3. Through a small gate, cross the usually dry bed of the **River Manifold** (if water is flowing, there are stepping stones just downstream) and climb to

a track on the far bank. Turn right and follow the track over a bridge spanning the tributary **River Hamps**. Keep going past a camping field to come out onto a lane at **Weag's Bridge**.

4. Signed to 'Thor's Cave', the **Manifold Way** continues opposite through a car park, alternately running through thick woodland and beside more-open meadows. After almost 1.6 kilometres/1 mile, you will arrive at a footbridge across the river beneath a towering crag, towards the top of which can be seen the yawning gape of **Thors Cave**.

Wetton's Victorian schoolmaster was an avid collector of fossils and other curiosities. From his finds of flint arrowheads, bronze jewellery and fragments of Romano-British pottery, he determined that the cave had been used by man throughout prehistory. He is buried in Wetton's churchyard, where his tombstone is carved with fossils.

5. Cross the **footbridge** and follow a broad path rising into the trees. At a junction partway up, turn sharp right along an intermittently stepped path that climbs to the huge mouth of the cave. It requires an easy scramble to get inside, but take care for the rock is smooth and can be slippery.

6. After exploring the cave, return to the top of the steps. However, instead of descending, walk

© Crown copyright and/or database right. All rights reserved. Licence number 100047867

High and dry: *Thor's Cave overlooks the Manifold Valley from a high rocky promontory*

forward on a path leading to a gate. Carry on across the head of a grassy fold, joining with the right-hand wall and shortly reaching a stile, just before a gate. Cross out onto a track and follow it left towards Wetton.

7. Coming out onto a lane, walk right to a junction and keep ahead into **Wetton** village. After 200 metres, turn off right to the **church**. Walk through the churchyard, emerging at the far side onto another lane. **Ye Olde Royal Oak** then lies just to the right. To complete the walk, continue beyond the pub to the next junction and turn right back to the car park. ♦

Thor's Cave

Thor's Cave and the soaring white cliff of Beeston Tor, were once easily accessible from the valley floor — which was originally much higher. The bones of wild animals long since extinct in Britain, such as woolly rhinoceros, bear and elk have been found in the cave. Oddest of all were some dolphin bones. Archaeologists suggest they may have been associated with an unknown Bronze Age religious cult.

Limestone cliffs loom above the path in Cales Dale

The Bull's Head
Monyash

What to expect:
Field paths and tracks; limestone dales and quarry paths

Distance/time: 8km/ 5 miles. Allow 2½ hours

Start: Monyash, village car park

Grid ref: SK 149 666

Ordnance Survey Map: Explorer OL24 Peak District: White Peak area: *Buxton, Bakewell, Matlock & Dove Dale*

The Pub: The Bull's Head, Church Street, Monyash, near Bakewell, DE45 1JH | 01629 812372 | www.thebullsheadmonyash.co.uk

Walk outline: From Monyash, the walk heads across the fields past disused lead workings to the old, monastic One Ash Grange Farm. Dropping through Cales Dale into the Lathkill Dale Nature Reserve, the route swings back past the source of the River Lathkill and abandoned quarry workings to the dry head of the dale before returning to the village.

Built as a farm in 1672, the Bull's Head is a traditional local at the heart of a thriving village. A highlight is the Spring Bank Holiday village well-dressing; the wells are blessed on the Saturday, while a Monday market on the green attracts stalls, a barbecue, and fun and games.

Bull's Head

▶ Bull's Head at a glance

Open: Mon-Thu 11.30am-3pm and 5.30-11pm; Fri-Sun and school holidays 11.30am-11pm

Brewery/company: Free house

Real ales: Black Sheep is always on tap together with three or four rotating guest ales that feature local micro-breweries

Food: Mon-Thu 11.30am-2pm and 5.30-9pm; Fri-Sun and school holidays 11.30am-9pm (Sat 9.30pm). All meals are home-made

Accommodation: None

Outside: Tables on patio and large beer garden at rear

Children & dogs: Good children and dogs on leads welcome

The Walk

1. Leaving the car park, head right, into the centre of the village. Go left past **The Bull's Head**, turning right beyond the end of the green into the churchyard. The path leads below the church tower, emerging at the far side of the graveyard onto a track. As you continue forward, glance right along **Icky Picky Lane** to see **Fere Mere**. *It is the last of four natural ponds that once furnished Monyash's water supply.*

Coming out onto a lane, go left. Keep ahead at two successive junctions into **Milkings Lane**, a walled track, signed 'The Limestone Way' that runs on between the fields.

2. At its end, a gate leads into pasture at the head of **Fern Dale**. Walk on by the right wall to pass through a gap stile. Bear left across rough grazing that is pitted with lead rakes, which in spring are rich in orchids and other wild flowers. Through a gate, carry on by the left wall, later slipping over a stile to continue on its opposite flank.

One Ash Grange soon appears ahead, the route eventually leaving the fields to follow a track down to the farm.

3. Approaching the buildings, fork left, passing a row of ancient pigsties. Just beyond is a **small cave** hewn from the rock, which served as an icehouse. Bear

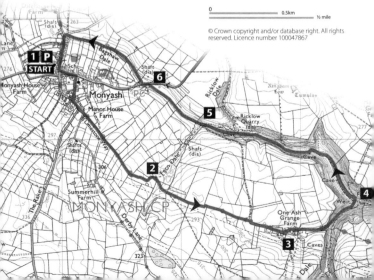

limestone dawn: *First light catches the lip of Upper Lathkill Dale*

ght between a large corrugated shed nd stone barn to a gate. Drop down teps and head away along the fold of he field. After another gate, the path rops through a **rocky cleft** and then uns along a terrace below a limestone liff. Reaching a junction, keep ahead long **Cales Dale** to reach **Lathkill Dale** t its foot.

. Cross a bridge over the **River Lathkill** nd turn left along the main dale. Beside he path, the river gurgles through a

strip of wetland where mallard often lurk in the vegetation. A little farther up, on the other side of the wall, is a resurgence, a spring bursting from a fissure beneath a rock. *Unless the weather has been particularly wet, the stream bed may be dry above that point. During springtime the rising banks of the valley are rich in wildflowers; cowslip, early purple orchid, speedwell and forget-me-not all being common. Higher up the valley, keep a look out for one of Derbyshire's rarer flowers, Jacob's ladder.*

The path meanders through the valley,

River bottom: *Crossing the River Lathkill*

passing an unnamed, but nonetheless impressive side dale. Just beyond there, on the left, is the opening of a **cave**, from which, after prolonged wet weather, the **River Lathkill** can gush out in a torrent. For most of the year, however, the river remains hidden below ground.

After crossing a wall, the valley closes in and its character suddenly changes. Bouldery mounds of stone from the **Ricklow Quarries** lie partly concealed by shrubs and trees, but even here, flowers such as water avens abound.

Before long, passing the foot of **Fern Dale**, the valley opens out once more.

5. To visit the **upper quarries**, from which there is a superb view back down the dale, double back sharp right on a stepped path. Occasional waymarkers confirm the route over a high shoulder and down to a gate. There, go right along a path that picks a way amongst the quarry waste and leads to a stunning **viewpoint above Lathkill Dale**. Although the path continues steeply down into the dale, the easiest option is to retrace your steps.

Back at (**5**), carry on at the base of the shallowing valley, soon leaving the

Lathkill Dale Nature Reserve. Keep going, before long, coming out onto a road.

6. Cross left to another path, which curves to a gate and stile below farm buildings. Walk on along **Bagshaw Dale** through a succession of small pastures, eventually emerging onto another lane at the edge of **Monyash**. Go left back into the village to complete the walk. ◆

Jacob's Ladder

With its spikes of striking blue flowers, Jacob's Ladder is to be found in only a handful of Derbyshire's dales. Flowering in June and July, it is particularly attractive to bees. The plant was known to the Greeks (its other name is Greek Valerian), who crushed the plant in wine to soothe toothache and insect bites. As recently as the nineteenth-century, physicians prescribed it to cure consumption (or tuberculosis) and syphilis.

Bakewell's honey-coloured limestone bridge and Georgian houses

The Peacock
Bakewell

What to expect:
Tracks, paths and a quiet lane; steep initial climb but more gentle descents

Distance/time: 11km/ 6¾ miles. Allow 3 hours

Start: Smith's Island long stay pay and display car park, Bakewell

Grid ref: SK 220 684

Ordnance Survey Map: Explorer OL24 Peak District: White Peak area: Buxton, Bakewell, Matlock & Dove Dale

The Pub: The Peacock, Bridge Street, Bakewell, Derbyshire DE45 1DS | 01629 813635 | www.peacockbakewell.com

Walk outline: Leaving the town, there is a steep climb to Manners Wood, where the path levels for a fine stretch through the trees. Doubling back over the ridge, the next section dips above the head of Calton, crossing another wooded spur before falling across Chatsworth Park to Edensor. The return follows an old greenway back over the hill, descending steeply through woodland and past the old station to the town.

Famous for its tarts, Bakewell maintains its tradition as a thriving market town and has no shortage of coaching inns and hotels to serve hungry passers-by. One to try is The Peacock in Market Street, just across the river from the car park.

The Peacock, Bakewell

▶ The Peacock at a glance

Open: Every day

Brewery/company: Free house

Real ales: Local Peak Ales, guest Adnams, continental beers

Food: The menu presents a mix of traditional pub favourites and chef's specials, all freshly prepared to order

Accommodation: Twin, double and family rooms

Outside: Patio garden with tables for when the sun shines

Children & dogs: Well-behaved children and dogs are welcome

The Walk

1. Turning right from the car park, cross a bridge and immediately go left, signed 'Monsal Trail'. At **Coombs Road**, swing right, but leave left after 175m along a drive. Fork right through a kissing gate and climb by the right boundary to a gate in the top corner.

2. Over a bridge, continue up the hill. Where the bounding fences end, cautiously proceed forward across a golf course fairway and climb beyond into the trees.

3. At a fork, just beyond a stream, bear right on a concessionary path through **Manners Wood**. The gradient now relents and the way rises easily through long established woodland. The understorey is rich in wildflowers during early spring, exploiting the abundance of light before the leaf canopy develops. After levelling near the top of the hill, the way gently loses height, progressing through beech and other deciduous trees into a plantation dominated by conifers.

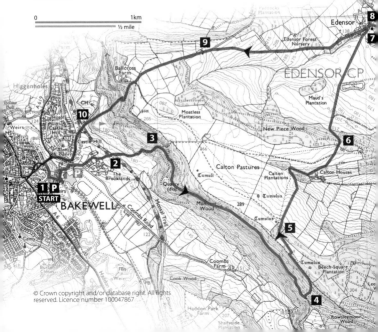

Early summer: *An unsurfaced lane lined with tall cow parsley, near Edensor*

4. Reaching a junction, turn sharp left and head up the hill. The trail soon levels beside a stone wall running along the crest of the ridge. Keep going, shortly passing through a gateway and later curving away to descend to a stile at the edge of the wood.

5. Keep ahead past a waypost, following a green trod down the open hillside of **Calton Pastures**, the gradient steepening as it approaches the **Calton Plantations**. Pass through a gate and

swing right beside the wall bounding the trees. Ignore a second gate lower down, staying with the now rising track. After 200 metres, the path moves away from the wall, climbing across the slope to a gate at the edge of **New Piece Wood**.

6. Follow a broad track between the trees. Emerging beyond onto the open parkland of the **Chatsworth estate**, head straight down the hill. Stay to the left of two successive stands of trees and then aim just left of the spire of **St Peter's Church** as it comes into view.

Sunlight and shadow: *Fragrant bluebells carpet the open glades in Manners Wood*

Keep an eye open too for roe deer, which graze amongst the sheep.

7. Reaching the edge of the park, leave by a metal gate tucked near the corner, from which a stepped path winds down between cottages to come out in the village. *To the right is the church, designed by Sir Gilbert Scott, and an extensive graveyard in which lie the bodies of Sir Joseph Paxton, who was head gardener at Chatsworth and designed the Crystal Palace, and Kathleen Kennedy, President Kennedy's sister who married the 10th Duke of Devonshire's eldest son William.*

You will also find the **Tea Cottage**, a great place to stop for afternoon tea.

8. Retrace your steps past the church but now continue along the rising lane through the village. At a junction where the tarmac ends, keep ahead with an old green lane, *its banks profuse in a variety of wildflowers such as stitchwort, bluebell, celandine, forget-me-nots and cow parsley. The increasing height opens views back across* **Chatsworth Park**.

9. Emerging onto a lane, head uphill. At a bend beyond the crest, bear left along an old, descending bridleway into trees. Lower down, cross a track and proceed cautiously over the golf course. Beyond

another crossing track, emerge onto a lane and turn left.

10. Reaching the main road, turn left. Immediately over the bridge, double back left on a riverside path. After 75 metres, a path off right leads into **Market Square** beside **The Peacock**. Otherwise, keep ahead to a footbridge, which crosses the **Wye** back to **Smith's Island car park**. ◆

Toxic beauty

Bluebells are a common woodland plant. They flower in April and May to form swathing carpets of delicate blue, their presence often indicating long-established or ancient woodland. When crushed, the bulbs produce a sticky substance that Tudors used for starching ruffs. It worked equally well as a glue; securing flights onto arrows for fletchers and was favoured by bookbinders: for, being toxic, it discouraged bookworm.

Woodland path beside the Goit

The Bridge Inn
Calver

What to expect:
Riverside and field paths and tracks; two steady ascents

Distance/time: 7.5km/ 4¾ miles. Allow 2½ hours

Start: The Bridge Inn, Calver, roadside parking by the old bridge

Grid ref: SK 247 744

Ordnance Survey Map: Explorer OL24 Peak District: White Peak area: *Buxton, Bakewell, Matlock & Dove Dale*

The Pub: The Bridge Inn, Calver Bridge, Hope Valley, Derbyshire S32 3XG | 01433 630415 | www.bridgeinncalver.co.uk

Walk outline: After heading upstream to New Bridge, the route rises over Hare Knoll and climbs through the old village of Calver. The trail then continues across the flank of Calver Peak, skirting the top edge of North Cliff Plantation before des cending along a quarry track to the road. The walk winds back by way of Bramley Wood and Bramley Farm, finally dropping to follow the Derwent back to the start.

Originally owned by the Duke of Rutland and dating to the 17th century, the pub has had only five landlords since 1920. It effuses a cosy atmosphere, with log fires adding a cheery warmth in winter.

Finest ales

▶ **The Bridge Inn at a glance**

Open: Daily from noon

Brewery/company: Ex Hardy & Hansons, now Greene King

Real ales: Three traditional hand-pulled ales including Abbot Ale, Old Golden Hen and Hardys & Hansons Bitter

Food: Mon-Sat: noon - 2.30pm and then 6-9pm, Sun: noon – 5pm. Dishes include local lamb and beef, salmon and crayfish.

Accommodation: None

Outside: Large beer garden overlooking the river

Children & dogs: Well behaved children and dogs always welcome

The Walk

1. Briefly walk west from the **old bridge** before turning right beside **Calver Mill Gallery** along a track to 'New Bridge' and 'Froggatt'. Go past Calver Mill's entrance to **Stocking Farm**, an attractive bow-fronted building whose adjacent barn once served as both a chapel and school. Wind to the right before the barn and then immediately left through a gate. Strike away across a pasture to meet **The Goit**, an artificial channel cut to bring water from a weir upstream to the mill. A track runs on below a wooded bank, emerging past cottages overlooking the weir onto the main road at **New Bridge**.

2. *To lengthen the walk through a small* **nature reserve** *by 1.5 kilometres/1 mile, cross the bridge and drop left onto a riverside path. Continue upstream, in time coming out onto a lane. Go left to a junction and then left again over* **Froggatt Bridge**. *Crossing a stile on the left, head downstream through the nature reserve. The path eventually winds right to a bridge spanning* **Stoke Brook**. *Return to the river and climb back to the road beside* **New Bridge**.

Now, take a path leaving the road over a stile that stands beside the end of the track by which you first arrived at **New Bridge**. Head up through trees to a stile

0 _____ 0.5km
        ½ mile

Ne'er cast a clout?: *Hawthorns or 'Muy' in bloom on the track up to Calver Peak*

into a field. Strike a shallow diagonal up to a gateway in the far corner. Carry on by the left wall, turning within the corner towards a derelict barn. Slip over a stile just before it and continue on the opposite side of the wall. Walk on in the next field to another stile at the top and turn left along the edge of a wood. At the wall's end, go sharp right on a descending track that finishes at the main road.

3. Opposite, **Donkey Lane** leads into the old village of **Calver**. At a junction go left, following the street around to a small square centred upon the base of an old cross, a stone water cistern and a memorial lamppost. Turn right, climbing **High Street** to the main road. *Partway up, notice three large water troughs on the left, tucked beneath a stone arch supporting the garden above.*

4. Cross the main road to a stile opposite and climb steeply away to the left. Meeting the sharp bend of a track, continue up the hill. Where the

Fields of glory: *Buttercups light up the fields overlooked by distant Curbar Edge*

track later swings right, keep ahead on a trod across the pasture, aiming for a stile at the top corner of a wood. Passing one of the **lead mines** that brought wealth to Calver during the 17th and 18th centuries, carry on above the trees. Through a gate keep going within the fringe of the trees, emerging at the far side to cross a bracken meadow. Walk out to a track and follow it down to a road.

5. The lane opposite rises gently into **Bramley Wood**. Where it then crests, leave left on a path at the top edge of the trees. Views open across to the Chatsworth estate, where the house and hunting tower can be made out. Before long, the path burrows through a rhododendron copse and loses height to a junction.

Go right, up to a stile. Head out to the far-left corner of a large field and, through a couple of gates, maintain the same diagonal line in a second field. Finally, pass through consecutive small enclosures to come out onto a lane beside **Bramley Farm**.

6. Walk down the hill for 400 metres/¼ mile before leaving beside a pair of large

double gates on the left. Head away on a trod, passing through a gap stile and then a gate to continue on a path below a wooded bank. Later, closing with the river, pass through a squeeze stile out of the wood and carry on at the edge of meadow. Remain beside the river, eventually crossing **Culver Sough**. A metalled path continues behind houses and underneath the main road to emerge by the old bridge opposite **Calver Mill Gallery** ♦

Colditz Castle?

Calver's cotton mill was built in 1778 and soon enlarged, but disaster struck when a flood took away the bridge in 1799 and again shortly after when fire swept through. Rebuilt in 1805, the mill continued working until 1923, and escaped eventual demolition by conversion into apartments. The mill is most famously known for its role as Colditz Castle in the 1970s BBC television series.

Peter's Stone dominates lovely Cressbrook Dale

The Bull's Head Inn
Foolow

What to expect:
*Field paths and tracks
with one ascent; short
section on quiet lane*

Distance/time: 9km/ 5½ miles. Allow 3 hours

Start: Foolow, roadside parking around village green

Grid ref: SK 190 768

Ordnance Survey Map: Explorer OL24 Peak District: White Peak
area: *Buxton, Bakewell, Matlock & Dove Dale*

The Pub: The Bull's Head Inn, Foolow, near Eyam, Hope Valley,
Derbyshire S32 5QR | 01433 630873 | www.thebullatfoolow.co.uk

Walk outline: Leaving the village green, field paths take
the route past the foot of Silly Dale to the main road at
Wardlow Mires. After descending into Cressbrook Dale, the
walk climbs onto higher ground at Wardlow. Expansive
views accompany the circuitous return across pastures and
the edge of moorland to The Bull's Head Inn at Foolow.

*Claimed to be one of the oldest pubs in the Peak, The Bull's
Head Inn was once a coaching stop along the Sheffield-
Buxton turnpike, routed through the village in 1793 to avoid
Eyam ridge. Inside are pack-saddles and the original bull's
head, while a ladder rises from the stables to a hayloft above.*

The bull's head

▶ The Bull's Head Inn at a glance

Open: Tue-Sat 12-3pm and 6.30-11pm, Sun 12-11pm, closed Mon
except Bank Holidays)

Brewery/company: Free House

Real ales: Four hand-pulled ales feature local breweries such as
Bradfield, Peak Ales and Abbeydale

Food: Available Tue-Sat 12-2pm and 6.30-9pm, Sun 12-2pm and
6-8pm. Pub and restaurant menus use local produce

Accommodation: Three comfortable rooms, one with a four-poster

Outside: Forecourt tables overlook the village green and pond

Children & dogs: Children and well behaved dogs always welcome

The Walk

1. From the green, pass left of the **duck pond** and leave at the corner along a walled path signed to 'Silly Dale'. Wind between houses to emerge in a narrow field. Look for a stile about one-third the way along on the left. Strike a right diagonal across a succession of meadows, eventually meeting a walled track. Cross and continue on the same heading, shortly coming out onto another track at the foot of **Silly Dale**.

2. Follow it to the right, passing a junction and curving out to the end of a lane by **Stanley House**.

3. Over a stile opposite, strike diagonally from the corner towards **Somerset House Farm**. Wind through the farmyard to emerge onto the main road opposite the **Yondermann Café.** Turn right past the **Three Stags Heads Inn**.

4. About 100 metres beyond the B6465, leave through a squeeze stile on the left. Walk directly away to a gap in the far wall. Through the gap go right to follow the base of the developing **Cressbrook Dale**. Keep right at a fork to wind below **Peter's Stone**, later passing stepping stones at the foot of **Tansley Dale**.

5. At a fork 30 metres later, bear left and climb past fenced off lead pits. Towards the top, watch for another

fork and keep left, climbing steeply to a gap stile in the top wall. If you reach a wooden gate you've gone too far; if so, double back left by the top wall to the squeeze stile.

6. Head along a walled track, winding beside a cottage onto the road at **Wardlow**. Turn right, uphill, leaving after 300 metres through a stile on the left.

7. Bearing right, contour across the slope, converging walls eventually ushering you to a gate. Maintain the same direction across two more fields to emerge onto a lane. Through a gate opposite, walk away by the left wall at the edge of **Longstone Moor**. After 500 metres, look for a stile on the left.

8. Head for another stile in the far wall and keep

Rising damp?: *Spring waters emerge at the surface after prolonged rainfall*

your heading over two more pastures to meet a narrow lane. Cross to a gate opposite and bear left past the **spoil heap** of an old mine. Through a gap in a wall, carry on across more fields in a northerly direction, ultimately coming out onto another lane.

9. Regain the fields diagonally opposite and continue the same line, crossing the access drive to **Castlegate Farm**. Keep going, skirting the corner of a wood to a pair of gates. Scale a stile beside the one on the right and resume your northerly heading across the fields to **Housley House**. There emerging onto the main road, cross to the lane opposite. Bear left at a junction to return to Foolow. ◆

Flower-rich limestone grassland

Unimproved limestone grasslands are one of the richest wildflower environments in Britain and steep meadows and the overgrown banks of old lanes are particularly resplendent. Cranesbill, harebell and scabious are everywhere, while carpets of rock rose spill across the slopes of Cressbrook Dale. The flowers in turn encourage butterflies such as brimstones, skippers, small heaths and brown Argus, whose larvae feed upon the rock rose.

A forgotten millstone decorates the path in Padley Gorge

The Grouse Inn
Nether Padley

What to expect:
Field and woodland paths; riverside path and wooded gorge

Distance/time: 9.5km/ 6 miles. Allow 3 hours

Start: Hay Wood National Trust pay and display car park, off A625

Grid ref: SK 255 777

Ordnance Survey Map: Explorer OL 24 Peak District: White Peak area: *Buxton, Bakewell, Matlock & Dove Dale* AND Explorer OL1 The Peak District: Dark Peak area: *Kinder Scout, Bleaklow, Black Hill & Ladybower Reservoir*

The Pub: The Grouse Inn, Nether Padley, Longshaw, Sheffield, S11 7TZ | 01433 630423 | www.thegrouseinn-derbyshire.co.uk

Walk outline: The route drops through Hay Wood to the River Derwent, following it upstream to Coppice Wood. Climbing back through the trees, it crosses the railway and continues into Grindleford. Turning up above Burbage Brook, the way climbs through Padley Gorge, emerging at the top into the Longshaw estate. It is then a pleasant stroll through the park to the Grouse Inn and the car park.

Starting out as an early 19th-century farm, The Grouse Inn soon began selling its own beer, taking its name from the birds on the Duke of Rutland's moor. Run for the last 50 years by the same family, it offers a welcoming finish to a day's walking.

Sunny beer garden

▶ **The Grouse Inn at a glance**

Open: Mon-Fri 12-3pm and 6-11pm

Brewery/company: Free house

Real ales: Four hand-pulled ales including Bank's, Marstons Pedigree, EPA and a local guest beer as well as whiskeys and wines

Food: Available Tue-Sat 12-2.30pm (3pm Sat) and 6.15-9pm, lunchtime only on Mon 12-2.30pm, but all day Sun 12-9pm

Accommodation: Self-catering cottage sleeping four

Outside: Attractive terrace patio looks out across Nether Padley

Children & dogs: Children and dogs welcome in separate room

Green velvet: *Mossy boulders strew the woodland floor in Padley Gorge*

The Walk

1. A sign from the car park marks the way over a crossing path to 'Nether Padley'. Head down across the steep, wooded slope of the hill. At a fork, branch left. Ignoring a crossing path lower down, drop to the corner of a wall and carry on with it on your right. Shortly leaving the trees, meet a track and go right. It winds out to the main road at the edge of **Nether Padley**.

2. Go right past **St Helen's Church**, crossing to a gate from which a path is signed to 'Leadmill' and 'Hathersage'. Follow the left boundary through an opening into a second field beside the **River Derwent**. Walk the length of the pasture, exiting at the far right corner over a bridge spanning the foot of **Burbage Brook**.

Through a gate, bear left to a stile and gate into the next field and continue beside the river, eventually passing into **Coppice Wood**. Keep going for another 400 metres/¼ mile to a junction.

3. Turn sharp right on a climbing path signed to 'Grindleford Station'. Entering the corner of a meadow, walk forward by the left boundary and then turn left across a bridge over the **railway line**. Bearing right, pass below the corner of a wall and carry on up to intercept a crossing track.

4. To the right the track leads towards **Grindleford**. Later, at a fork, keep left to walk past **Padley Chapel** and **Brunt Barn**. Keep going for a further 400 metres/¼ mile beyond a row of houses to a junction.

5. Grindleford Station and its café lie a short distance ahead, but the onward route is to the left, signed 'Longshaw Estate via Padley Gorge'. The track climbs steeply away, passing through a gate into the oak and birch woodland of the gorge. *Higher up as the gradient eases, look left to see a curious small building set back amongst the trees. It served to store explosives*

for use in the Bole Hill quarries in the hill behind.

After briefly dropping the path resumes a gradual ascent. Disregard a path later signed off to 'Surprise View' and 'Bole Hill Quarry' and eventually emerge at the top of the wood onto **open heath**. Closing with the stream, ignore the first bridge and continue a little farther to a **second bridge**.

6. Cross and follow a path signed to 'Longshaw Visitor Centre' that slants up

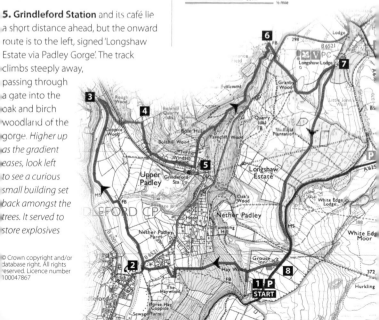

Rocky river: *The tumbled boulders in Padley Gorge are testimony to the power of water*

to the road. Through a gate opposite, the way winds around a **restored barn** and on at the edge of **Granby Wood**, named for the Marquis of Granby, the Duke of Rutland's son. Passing through gates, skirt a **pond**, and carry on through rhododendron coppice and then at the edge of **Longshaw Meadow**. Continue above a ha ha beside more rhododendron bushes to a junction within a clump of yew trees.

7. The path through the gate ahead leads to the **Longshaw National Trust Visitor Centre and tearoom**. However, the onward route lies through the gate on the right, joining a drive from the lodge. Heading across the park, look for an abandoned millstone on the left and keep your eye open for the fallow deer that roam free. Farther on, near a pair of redundant gateposts is a sculpted stone, one of twelve scattered across the Derbyshire Peak in an open-air art project.

At a crossing, where the way ahead is signed to the 'Grouse Inn', the Totley railway tunnel burrows some 140 metres beneath your feet. Keep with the main drive, which ultimately ends through

a gate onto the A625. Go right to the **Grouse Inn**.

8. Emerging from the pub, turn right, leaving the road almost immediately over a stile on the right. A diagonal trod strikes from the corner across successive meadows to the edge of **Hay Wood**. Leaving the fields, walk left the short distance to the car park to complete the walk. ♦

Millstones

Derbyshire millstones have been produced since at least the mid-15th century, massive circular blocks weighing around three tons. Quarried and dressed by skilled hands, they could take a fortnight or more to make. Pairs were required for grinding grain, but single stones, rolled upright around a circular iron track, were used for crushing ore. Other stones were cut as grindstones and served the cutlery industry.

Wisps of low cloud roll over the heather on Abney Low

The Barrel Inn
Bretton

What to expect:
Rough field paths and open moorland; some steep ascents

Distance/time: 8km/ 5 miles. Allow 2½ hours

Start: The Barrel Inn, Bretton; roadside parking

Grid ref: SK 201 779

Ordnance Survey Map: Explorer OL24 Peak District: White Peak area: *Buxton, Bakewell, Matlock & Dove Dale*

The Pub: The Barrel Inn, Bretton, near Eyam, Hope Valley, Sheffield, South Yorkshire S32 5QD | 01433 630856 | www.thebarrelinn.co.uk

Walk outline: Leaving Eyam Ridge at Bretton, the route drops steeply into Bretton Clough, climbing across the flank of Abney Low to Abney. The return descends along Abney Clough into forest, crossing Highlow Brook at Stoke Ford before climbing onto the edge of Eyam Moor and a pleasant finish along an old lane back to the pub.

The highest inn in Derbyshire, the Barrel supposedly takes its name from a massive underground vault beneath the hill, created by miners digging for lead ore. The hilltop site looks out over five counties; fine ales and food, log fires and oak beams make it one not to miss.

Roll out the barrel?

▶ The Barrel Inn at a glance

Open: Mon-Fri 12-3pm and 6-11pm, Sat and Sun all day from noon

Brewery/company: Free house

Real ales: Four hand-pulled ales feature favourites such as IPA, Hardy and Hanson, Marstons Pedigree, with a rotating guest ale.

Food: Available Mon-Sat 12-2pm and 6-9pm, Sun 12-9pm. Wherever possible, food is locally sourced to produce a changing menu of mouth-watering snacks and full meals.

Accommodation: Three twin/double and one family room

Outside: Tables overlook one of the best panoramas in the Peaks

Children & dogs: Children and well-behaved dogs welcome

The Walk

1. Turn down the narrow lane beside the pub. After 400 metres/¼ mile, as it then bends right, leave ahead on a narrow path beside a cottage. Go through a small gate at the bottom and continue down to a stile. The ongoing path drops left across the steep slope of the wooded valley. Approaching a bench, bend sharp right, swinging left lower down above a stream. Through a gate, keep ahead on a lesser path, emerging from the trees and shortly reaching a junction.

2. Go right through a break in a wall, the trod winding on across rough pasture. As it then begins to rise beside a broken wall, bear left below the ruin

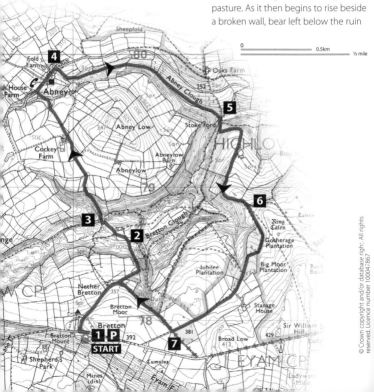

Valley view: *Looking towards Smelting Hill from the path above Bretton Clough*

of a farmstead. Cross a second broken wall and walk forward. Within 10 metres, branch left to stepping-stones across a stream. Climb beyond to a path and follow it right, but then fork right again to cross another stream near a solitary oak. Turn right once more, walking down above the stream to a plank bridge spanning **Bretton Brook**.

3. Through a small gate, the onward path is discretely signed to 'Abney'. Over a second bridge, gain height across the steep bracken-covered slope of the valley, the path eventually levelling to a stile. Cross a stream and swing right alongside a wall. At the field corner, mount a stile beside a gate and carry on to another stile. Bear right to a track and follow it past **Cockey Farm**.

Where the track then bends left, keep ahead at the field edge. After 100 metres, watch for a stile and kissing-gate. Strike out on a sharp left diagonal, dropping at the far side to a stream. Cross and continue on a contouring path above the stream to a small gate.

Green on green: *From the path a broad panorama opens over Bretton Clough*

Drop to a plank bridge and climb away left, passing out through a gate onto a lane. Turn right through **Abney**.

4. After 250 metres, bear off right along a descending track, which soon narrows to a path. Through a gate, carry on down at the edge of scrub and grazing above **Abney Brook**. Passing through gates, the ongoing path eventually enters a wood and continues delightfully though **Abney Clough**. Emerging from the trees at a junction, go right towards Bretton. Cross **Abney Brook** and pass through

a gate to a bridge spanning **Bretton Brook** beside **Stoke Ford**.

5. Take the rising path opposite signed to 'Grindleford'. Shortly reaching a fork, branch left, climbing from the trees through bracken and heather. After a stiff pull, the path curves to run beside a wall. Cross a stile beside a rusting gate and continue up more easily by the wall to another gate and stile.

6. Cross and turn right to carry on with the wall now on your right, before long passing **Gotheridge Plantation**. Eventually reaching a gate and stile, cross and walk away beside the right

wall. Ignore a later stile onto access land and keep going to a field gate and stile. Continue ahead to join a track from **Stanage House Farm**, which leads out to a crossing of tracks.

7. Turn right at the edge of **Duric Common**. Reaching a cottage at **Nether Bretton** the track becomes metalled, swinging left and finally leading back to the **Barrel Inn**. ♦

Bretton Clough

Cleaving the limestone plateau, Bretton Clough is a surprisingly wild and seemingly remote valley, and served to hide cattle from marauding troops supporting Bonnie Prince Charlie's unsuccessful claim to the throne in 1745. But there were once several farmsteads in the valley, one of which established warrens to breed rabbits for their fur. The enterprise proved unsuccessful, but their burrowing destabilised the shale banks of the valley side.

Setting out on the path up Grindbrook Clough

The Old Nag's Head
Edale

What to expect:
Rugged but well-used hill paths with a long ascent and descent; several stream crossings

Distance/time: 10km/ 6¼ miles. Allow 3½-4 hours

Start: Edale pay and display car park

Grid ref: SK 123 853

Ordnance Survey Maps: Explorer OL1 The Peak District: Dark Peak area: Kinder Scout, Bleaklow, Black Hill & Ladybower Reservoir

The Pub: The Old Nag's Head, Edale, Hope Valley, Derbyshire S33 7ZD | 01433 670 291 | www.the-old-nags-head.co.uk

Walk outline: The walk begins through Edale, then climbs beside Grinds Brook Clough onto the edge of the moor. The way cuts behind Grindslow Knoll to join the edge above Crowden Brook. After an initial steep descent into the valley, the path accompanies the stream to the farm at Upper Booth. The return contours below Broadlee Bank Tor back to the Old Nag's Head at Edale.

The Old Nag's Head has been a focus of Edale's scattered community for centuries and is listed as one of the best 100 pubs in England. When the Pennine Way was officially opened in 1965, the inn was adopted as the official start of the walk.

One for the Pennine Way?

▶ The Old Nag's Head at a glance

Open: Daily from noon

Brewery/company: Dorbiere Pub Group

Real ales: Selection of four hand-pulled ales, including a local guest beer and another specially brewed for the pub, 'Nag's 1577'

Food: Every day from noon until 9.30pm (8pm Sun). Great range of traditional pub food. Children's portions and vegetarian menu, too

Accommodation: Two nearby self-catering cottages

Outside: Sheltered beer garden behind the pub

Children & dogs: Children, dogs and muddy boots all welcome

The Walk

1. Leaving the car park near the toilets, follow the lane beneath a **railway bridge** and up past the **church** into the scattered hamlet of **Edale**. Keep ahead past the **Old Nag's Head**, the lane shortly degrading to gravel.

2. Reaching the **lodge gate to Grindslow House**, bear right off the track onto a path signed to 'Grinds

Brook'. Drop across the stream and climb the steep bank beyond. A flagged causey leads away to the left at the edge of open pasture below **The Nab**. In time the way passes through a small **wood**, coming out at the far side to a bridge spanning a stream falling from **Golden Clough**.

3. A broad path continues along the

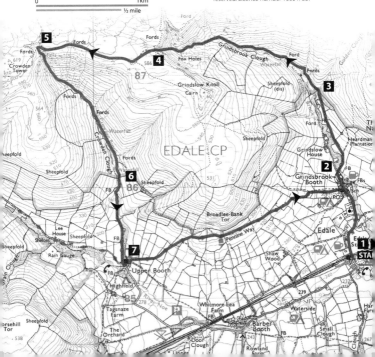

Beautiful bridge: *A lovely artisan's bridge spans Golden Clough*

hillside into the valley, later closing with the stream and becoming more rugged. After rising over a bluff, the path returns to the stream, swapping from one side to the other in search of the best route. Higher up, where the valley splits, stay with the left branch. The route clambers on over a tumble of rocks, eventually emerging at the top onto the edge of the moor by a large cairn.

4. To the left a flagged path cuts across the neck of **Grindslow Knoll**. As you wander on, there is a sense of the featureless emptiness that pervades this high plateau. The way later swings right above the steep slope of **Crowden Clough** to reveal a fine view across the Vale of Edale. Carry on for another 800 metres/½ mile past a couple of impressive outcrops before the path drops into a small amphitheatre, where rivulets draining from the moor merge at the head of **Crowden Brook**.

5. Cross the stream and take a path to the left above the deepening ravine.

Winding road: *Looking back down the meandering path beside Grindsbrook Clough*

As you then pass beneath the ragged cliffs of **Crowden Tower**, watch for a fork in the path. Take the left branch, which initially drops very steeply into the valley and requires care. Reaching the stream, as on the way up, the way alternates between the banks, but soon settles along the eastern flank. The path steadily improves, ultimately leaving the access land over a stile next to a gate.

6. Walk on beside the now wooded gully of the stream to a **bridge**. Climb out on the far side to continue at the edge of pasture. Over a stile and past a barn, the way winds between the trees lining the clough and finally meets a narrow lane at **Upper Booth**.

7. Go left over the bridge to the bus turning circle by a red telephone box and turn left into Upper Booth Farm. Follow the track through the yard, swinging right and then left to a junction. Branch right through a gate, the way signed as the 'Pennine Way' to Edale. A clear path leads on across the fields, shortly passing a derelict barn and then rising over a mound that has slumped beneath **Broadlee-Bank Tor**.

Through a gate at the top a splendid view opens ahead to Mam Tor and the Great Ridge. Keep going from field to field, the way becoming flagged and descending to a junction. Turn right beside a stream along a sunken path that leads into the village opposite the **Old Nag's Head**. Head back down the lane to the car park to complete the walk. ◆

The Pennine Way

Most people take around eighteen days to walk the 268-mile trail, but in 1989, Mike Hartley ran it in under two days 17½ hours. Conceived by Tom Stephenson in 1935, thirty years were to pass before the Pennine Way was officially opened. Following England's backbone to the Border Hotel in Kirk Yetholm, just across the Scottish border, it is regarded as one of the country's toughest long-distance walks.

LANTERN PIKE

Sunset reflected in the toposcope on the summit of Lantern Pike

The Lantern Pike Inn
Hayfield

What to expect:
Good field paths and tracks; sustained ascent but easy return

Distance/time: 7km/ 4½ miles. Allow 2½ hours

Start: Sett Valley Trail pay and display car park, Hayfield

Grid ref: SK 035 869

Ordnance Survey Map: Explorer OL1 The Peak District: Dark Peak *area: Kinder Scout, Bleaklow, Black Hill & Ladybower Reservoir*

The Pub: The Lantern Pike Inn, 45 Glossop Road, Little Hayfield, Derbyshire SK22 2NG | 01663 747590 | www.lanternpikeinn.co.uk

Walk outline: The walk follows the Sett Valley Trail to Birch Vale, where it then crosses the river and climbs steadily onto the top of Lantern Pike, which overlooks the town. The return drops steeply to the old mill village of Little Hayfield, where you will find the Lantern Pike Inn. It is then an easy stroll along a field track back to Hayfield.

Coronation Street hit the airwaves in December 1960, the first episodes penned in the Lantern Pike's own snug by a young Tony Warren. Inside, the walls are decorated with Corrie memorabilia, including the Newton and Ridley mirror and doors from the Rover's Return.

Rover's Return?

▶ The Lantern Pike Inn at a glance

Open: Mon from 5pm, Tue-Fri 12-3pm and from 5pm, Sat & Sun all day from noon

Brewery/company: Free house

Real ales: Timothy Taylor and guest beer from local micro-brewery

Food: Mid-week lunches 12-2.30pm (except Mon), evening meals 5-8pm (Mon and Tues) 5-8.30pm (Wed-Fri). At weekends, food is served all day from 12 until 9pm (Sat) or 8pm (Sun)

Accommodation: Five cosy twin or double rooms

Outside: Sheltered beer garden at rear with views to Lantern Pike

Children & dogs: Children welcome; kids' menu

The Walk

1. Leave the far end of the car park along a broad gravel track marked as the 'Sett Valley Trail'. It runs pleasantly along the valley side, where breaks in the trees give views across to Lantern Pike. After around 1.6 kilometres/1 mile, keep with the track as it winds to the right, emerging onto a lane at **Birch Vale**.

2. Turn down past the **Special Touch Café** and cross the **River Sett**. Just past a curving terrace of **mill cottages**, leave up a block stone track on the right signed the 'Pennine Bridleway to Lantern Pike'. A steady climb now sets the pace for the next leg of the walk. Passing through a gate to meet another track, keep heading up, shortly emerging onto a lane by more cottages.

3. Go right and immediately left into a narrow lane, signed again as the 'Pennine Bridleway'. Passing the top cottage, the surface degrades to gravel and continues rising to a gate at the edge of the National Trust's **Lantern Pike estate**.

If you have had enough climbing you can remain with the track, but you will miss the top of the hill. For that, immediately

0 _____ 1km
_____ ½ mile

River village: *Stone cottages line the River Sett in the heart of Hayfield village*

through the gate, turn off left on a path rising steeply beside the wall. At the crest, pause to take in the view and then go right, the path now running easily along the heathy spine of the hill. *Amongst the bilberry and heather are patches of cotton grass, selected as Greater Manchester's county flower in 2002. In spring, lapwings and skylarks take to the skies but keep an eye open on the ground too, for you might also see a mountain hare.*

4. Etched onto the summit topograph are the surrounding skyline landmarks. Notable to the east is the Kinder plateau while to the south is Axe Edge and Shining Tor. Continue along the descending ridge, in a little while the path steepening to rejoin the track that has come around the base of the hill. Leave the National Trust land through a gate and walk on across a stream to a vague fork. Bear left, following a trod to the distant corner of a rough pasture near **Blackshaw Farm**.

5. Double back sharp right beside the

Fields and dales: *A trod curves across the meadows from the hamlet of Little Hayfield*

bounding wall, the way signed to 'Little Hayfield'. The path runs along the side of a shallow ridge, giving views across the valley to Leygatehead Moor. Over a stile in the corner lose height across the steepening heath by the edge of **Hey Wood**, eventually arriving at an ivy-clad cottage. Cross its drive to the path diagonally opposite and continue down beside an old hedge. Swing left with the corner, descending to a causey, which leads down the hill to **Clough Mill**. Wind out over a couple of **bridges** onto a lane and go left past the mill entrance. Carry on a short distance beyond to a gap stile on the left. Drop across the stream to another lane in front of mill cottages. Go right to the main road and the **Lantern Pike Inn**.

6. Leaving the pub, follow the main road right across the stream. Just past another row of cottages, turn off right into **Slack Lane**. At the end of the houses, fork left through a gate along a path signed to 'Hayfield'. Emerging after 800 metres/½ mile onto a narrow lane by a cottage, go left and follow it out to a street at the edge of **Hayfield**.

7. Walk left, but after 100 metres, just before passing beneath a road bridge,

leave through a gate on the right at the start of the **Calico Trail**. Bear left across a recreation field, joining a riverside path to a **bridge**, just below the site of a former mill. Cross and follow a contained path, which winds out onto another street. Go left back to the car park to complete the walk. ♦

Trouble at t'mill

Clough Mill's opening around 1830 was met by rioting as home spinners protested against the end of their cottage industry. Trouble flared again when the American Civil War disrupted cotton imports during the 1860s. But, following a fire in 1870, it was largely rebuilt to run on steam and continued producing cotton until 1920. After housing other assorted industries, the mill was saved from demolition by being converted into apartments.

Boots Folly above the Loxley Valley, with Strines Reservoir below

The Old Horns Inn
High Bradfield

What to expect:
Woodland and field paths; a short but steep ascent

Distance/time: 6km/ 4¼ miles. Allow 2 hours

Start: The Sands car park, Low Bradfield

Grid ref: SK 262 920

Ordnance Survey Map: Explorer OL1 The Peak District: Dark Peak area: *Kinder Scout, Bleaklow, Black Hill & Ladybower Reservoir*

The Pub: The Old Horns Inn, High Bradfield, Sheffield, South Yorkshire S6 6LG | 0114 285 1207 | www.theoldhorns.co.uk

Walk outline: Overlooking the Loxley valley, Low and High Bradfield are disparate parts of a single village. From the low town, the walk rises beside the Agden Dam to the lake's western shore. Rounding its tip, the route climbs above the Agden Bog Nature Reserve to the valley rim. The return contours open hillside and woodland to the pub at High Bradfield, dropping back through fields to the start.

Two pubs once faced each other across the street, but only the Old Horns Inn, rebuilt in the late 19th century, remains. There is a stunning view from the terrace and the Inn has earned an enviable reputation for hospitality and excellent food.

Ideal for a mid-walk break

▶ The Old Horns Inn at a glance

Open: Daily from 11.30am

Brewery/company: Thwaites

Real ales: Eight hand-pulled cask ales which includes guest beers from the local Bradfield Brewery

Food: Superb value home-cooked food served Mon-Fri, 11.30am-3pm and 5-9pm, Sat 11.30am-9pm, Sun 11.30am-7pm. Specials boards, theme-menu nights and all-day traditional Sunday carvery

Accommodation: Eight en-suite rooms

Outside: Deck terrace with unrivalled view across the valley

Children & dogs: Children and dogs on leads always welcome

The Walk

1. Leaving the car park, follow the lane right up the hill. Take the next right, **Windy Bank**, and climb to the **Agden Dam**.

2. Leave through a gap in the bordering wall beside a small lay-by to follow a permissive path through the trees, initially beside the lakeshore and later rising higher across the bank. After 800 metres/½ mile, descend to a small gate and continue beyond the head of the reservoir to a footbridge. Climb the far bank to a track and turn right through the **Agden Bog Nature Reserve**.

If the permissive path is closed, stay with the lane for another 550 metres, eventually arriving at a gated track that branches off right. Running across the wooded slope of the hill, it shortly winds to a stone bridge high above **Emlin Dike**. Where the bounding walls subsequently end, turn right on a crossing path and follow it downhill to a stone bridge spanning **Agden Dike**. The track then bends right above the stream through the **Agden Bog Nature Reserve**.

3. Reaching a gate, pass through, but immediately turn sharp left up the edge of a felled and re-planted plot of woodland. At the corner, swing right within the wall boundary and resume the climb. Slip over a stile partway up and continue on the other side of the fence to the top of the hill.

4. A path leads away to the left beside a wall, giving a superb view across the heath and woodland of the

Rock of ages: *St Nicholas' Church at Higher Bradfield*

Agden valley. Later passing through a kissing-gate, the path bends right to meet a lane.

5. Cross to a ladder-stile and walk forward a few metres to a waypost. Turn right and head across the field, leaving over a stile next to a gate onto a second lane. Scale the stile opposite and head away along an old **green lane**. Beyond a stile at the bottom, the track curves right, descending beside **Sick Brook** to a ruined farmstead at **Rocher Head**.

Passing the buildings, the path winds right and then left. Continue along the valley side, keeping a sparse, outgrown hedge on your right.

6. Reaching a junction of paths by a redundant ladder-stile, wind right and left through the gap and resume your south-easterly course, the way signed to 'High Bradfield'. Shortly closing with a fence over to the left, cross a stile in a short stretch of wall and carry on above the head of a spring that falls into a wooded dell. A faint trod leads unerringly on, after a while reaching a wall gap. Drop right to a track beneath

Green and blue: *Looking down over stone walled pastures to the Agden Reservoir*

an ancient oak and go left, following it across **Rocher Brook**.

7. Passing through a gate into felled and re-planted woodland, climb away beside a broken wall. Through gateposts at the top, turn right and keep with the ongoing path along the side of the **Rocher End Valley**. Entering mature broad–leaved woodland, the path gently rises across the steep bank, eventually emerging at a junction of paths and squeeze stile. To the left is **Bailey Hill**, a motte and bailey,

possibly Saxon and whose mound and earthwork defences remain impressively visible. The onward path, however, lies through the squeeze stile into Bradfield's extended graveyard. Wind in front of **St Nicholas' Church** and leave by the main gate. **The Old Horns Inn** lies just ahead at the other end of the street.

8. Return to the churchyard gate, but go through the gate on the left. A contained path angles around the perimeter of the **old graveyard**. Through a gate at the far end, drop left down steps and bear right through an open gateway. Walk away at the field edge, continuing into a second field.

clear path soon develops, running above trees to a fence stile in the bottom corner. Go forward through a small metal gate out onto a lane. The footpath carries on opposite beside the grounds of a house. At the bottom, cross an overgrown track and continue down steps to a footbridge. Cross and follow the path downstream back to the car park. ♣

Agden Bog Nature Reserve

The nature reserve occupies the valley below Agden Side, where the birch woodland at the head of the reservoir gives way to heathery moor. Amongst the plants are crowberry and cranberry with flowers such as heath spotted orchid and the cuckoo flower, which attracts orange tip butterflies. Look out for two carnivorous plants too, common butterwort and sundew; both of which survive by trapping small insects.

Useful Information

Visit Peak District & Derbyshire

The Peak's official tourism website covers everything from accommodation and special events to attractions and adventure. **www.visitpeakdistrict.com**

Peak District National Park

The Peak District National Park website also has information on things to see and do, plus a host of practical details to help plan your visit. **www.peakdistrict.org**

Tourist Information Centres

The main TICs provide free information on everything from accommodation and transport to what's on and walking advice..

Bakewell	01629 816558	bakewell@peakdistrict.gov.uk
Castleton	01629 816572	castleton@peakdistrict.gov.uk
Moorland Centre	01433 670207	edale@peakdistrict.gov.uk
Upper Derwent	01433 650953	derwentinfo@peakdistrict.gov.uk

Bus Travel

Peakland's towns and many of the villages are served by bus. Information is available from Traveline on 0871 200 22 33 or **www.traveline.info**

Peak District breweries and pubs

As well as the bigger Peak District breweries such as Marstons or Timothy Taylor, the area supports more than twenty microbreweries producing award-winning real ales and craft beers plus a handful of real cider and perry makers.

For details of the encouragingly high number of real ale pubs in the Peak District, see the local CAMRA websites, or buy a copy of their excellent, annual *Good Beer Guide.*

Visitors can also sample a mouth-watering range of local real ales at the many Peak District beer festivals held throughout the year.

For details, see: **www.camra.org.uk, www.derbycamra.org.uk, www.sheffieldcamra. org.uk** or **www.hpneccamra.org.uk**

Weather

Online weather forecasts for the Peak District are available from the Met Office at **www.metoffice.gov.uk/loutdoor/mountainsafety/** and the Mountain Weather Information Service at **www.mwis.org.uk/**